Tapestry
of
Florals

ELIZABETH ELIUK

Tapestry of Florals

ISBN 978-1539917427

Graphic design by Ingénieuse Productions
Edmonton, Alberta, Canada

Tapestry of Florals
AN ARTIST'S PERSPECTIVE

To colour your own tapestry
and create your own
stress-free perspective

Artist's Statement

All designs are modified from the artist's original artwork.
Designed especially for you to colour your own tapestry from
your own perspective!
Enjoy using your choice of any colour pencil brand, crayons,
markers or whatever combination works for you!

—Elizabeth Eliuk

www.facebook.com/people/Elizabeth-Eliuk/100011777359791

www.artwanted.com/artist.cfm?ArtID=85552

fineartamerica.com/artists/elizabeth+eliuk

www.artblr.com/elizabetheliuk1470590345

elizabetheliuk.pixels.com/

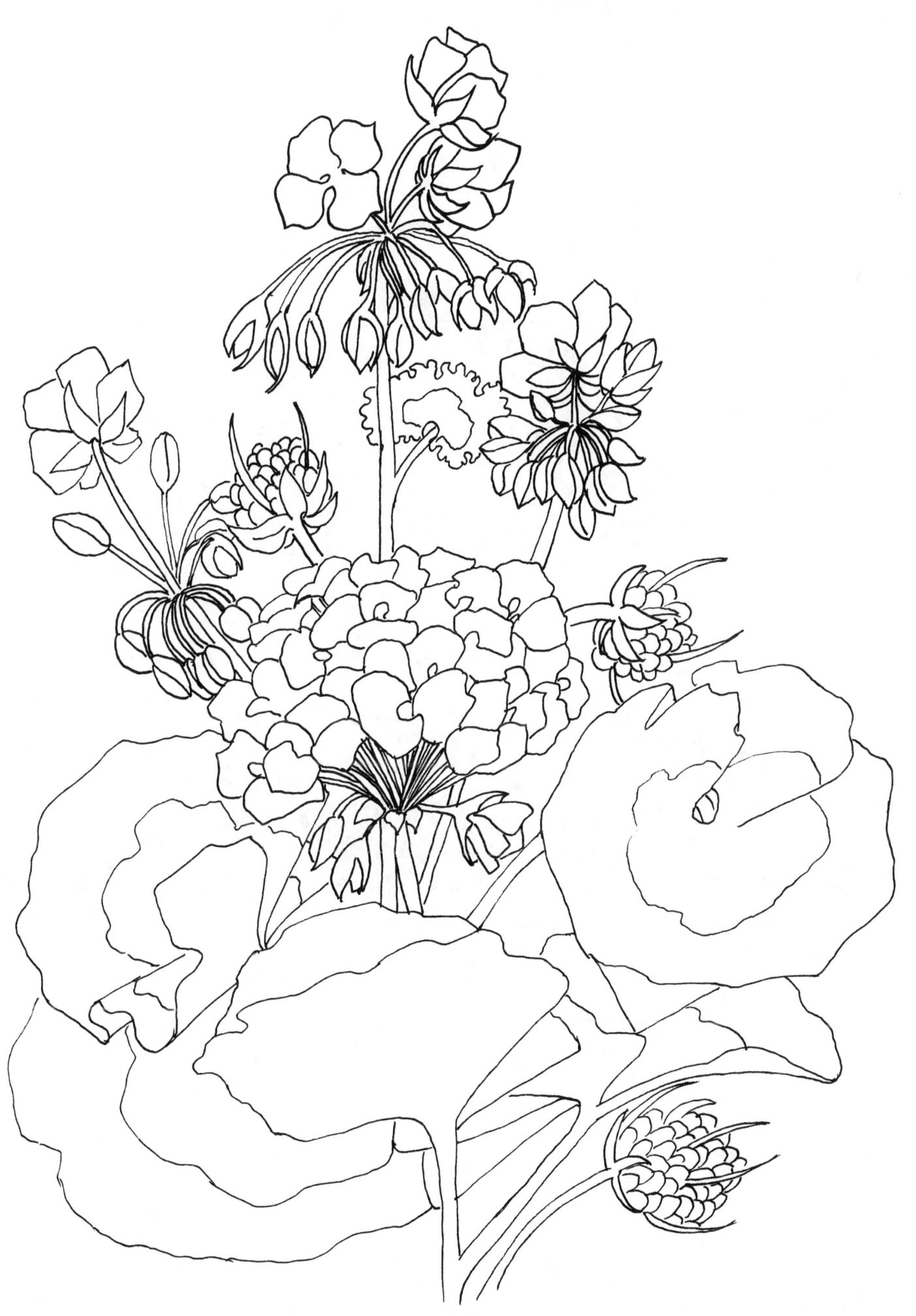

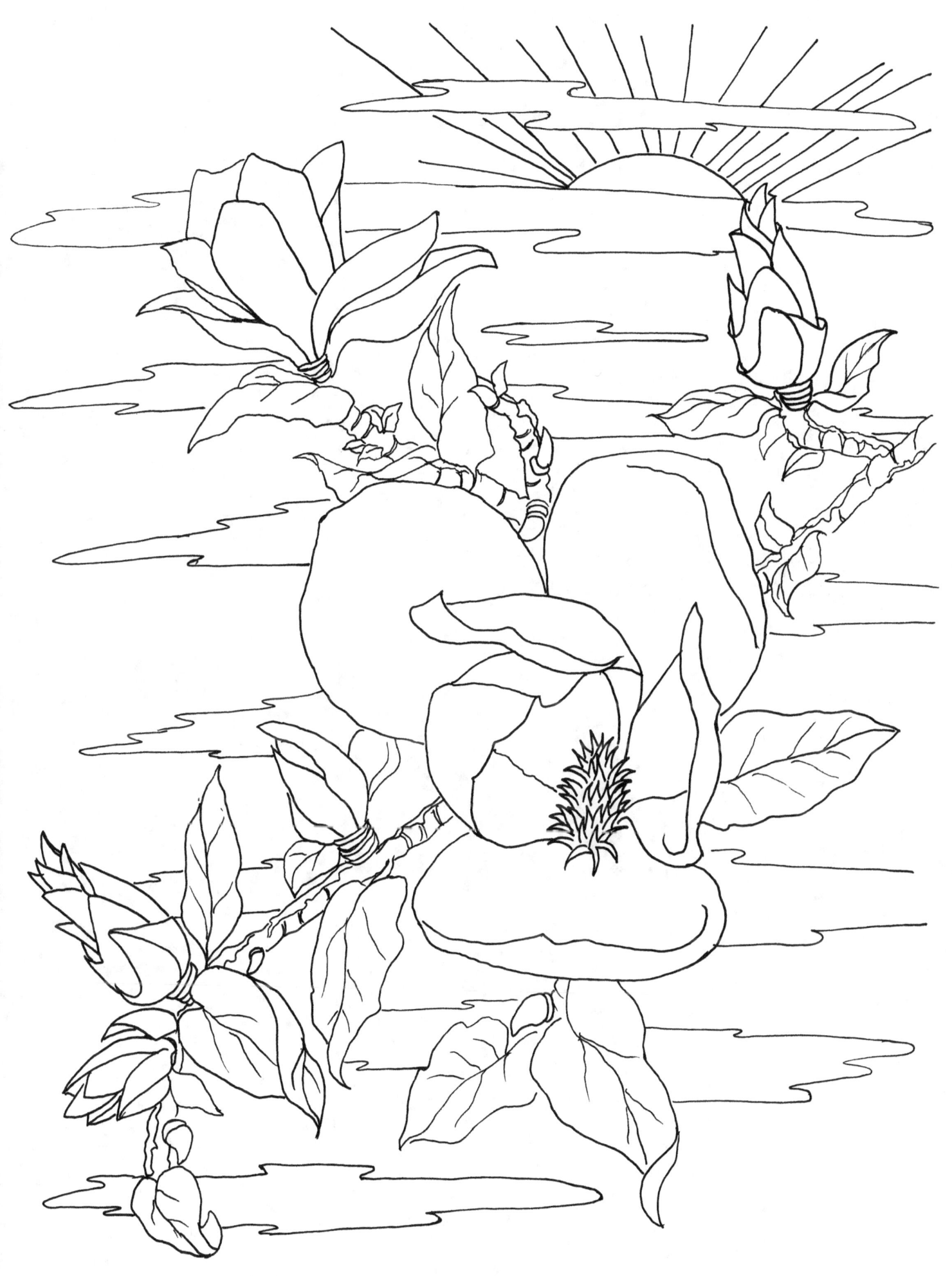

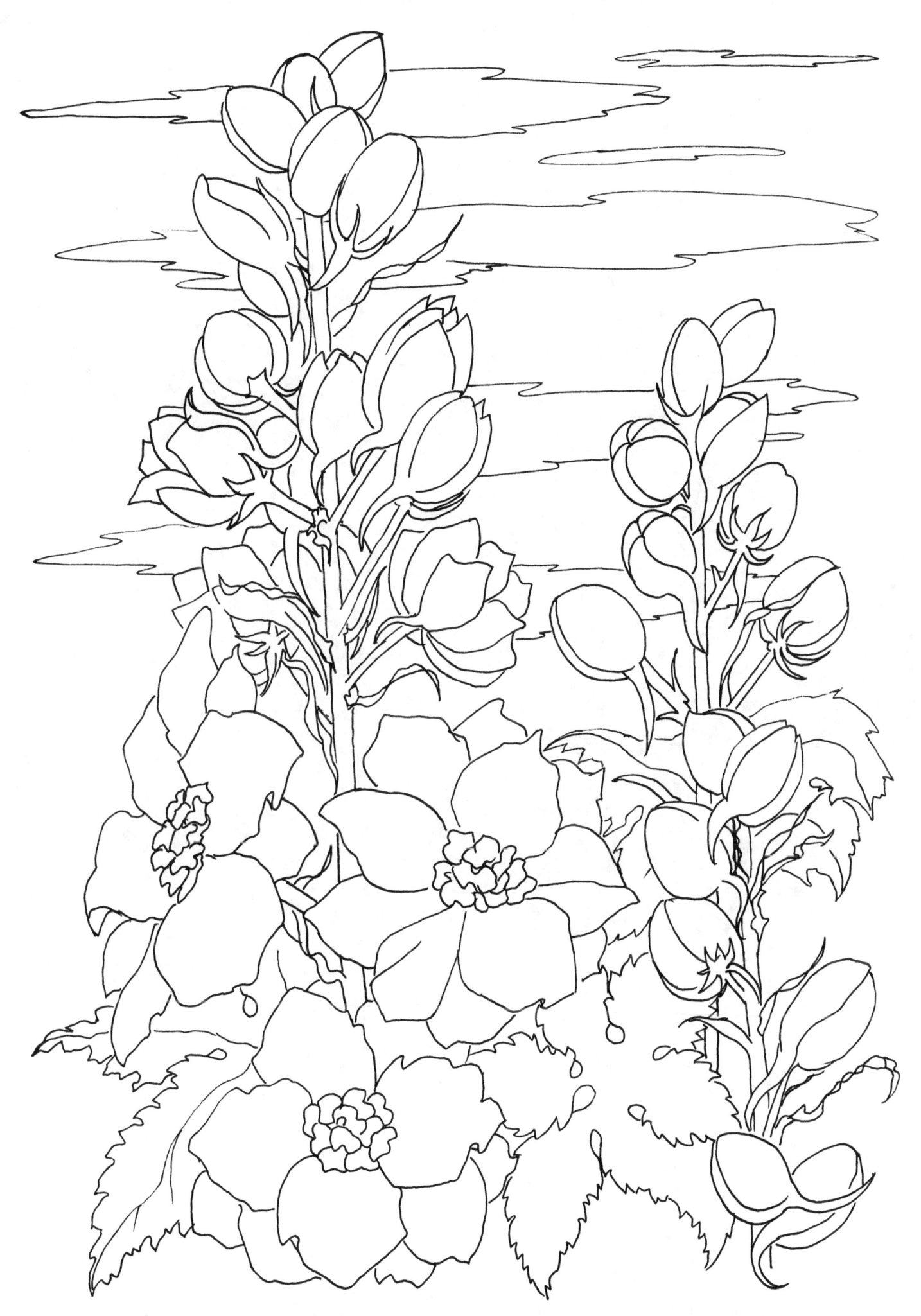

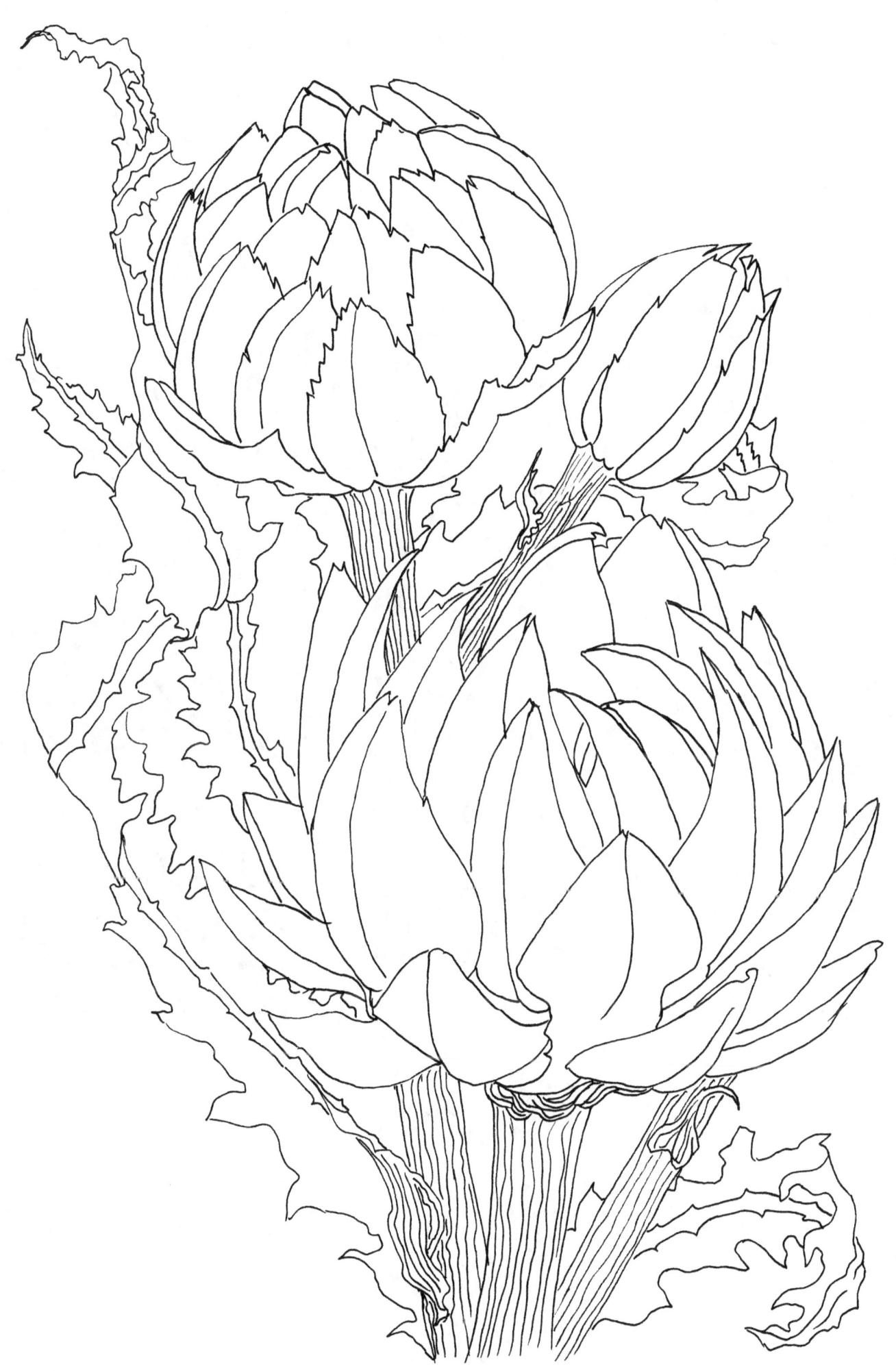

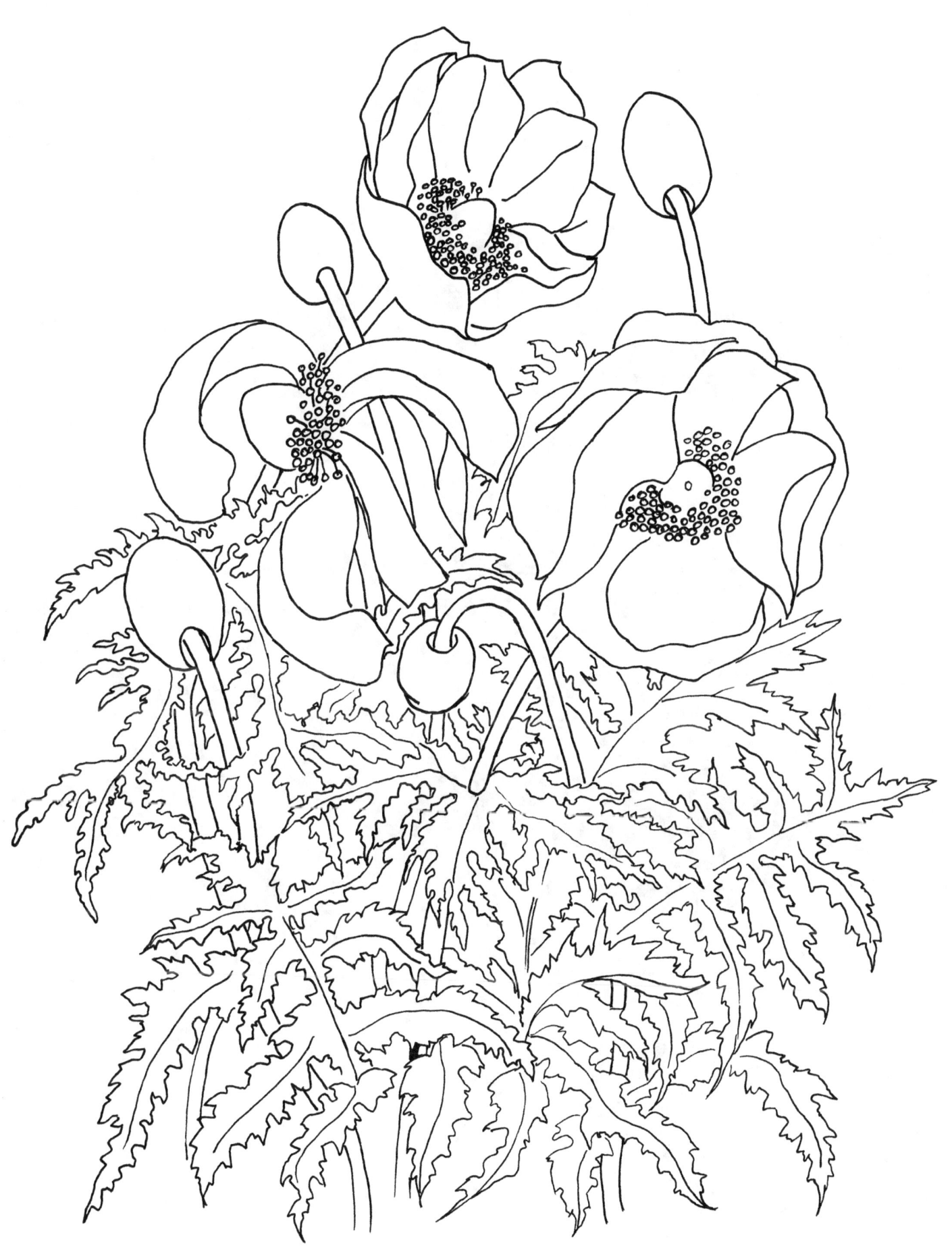

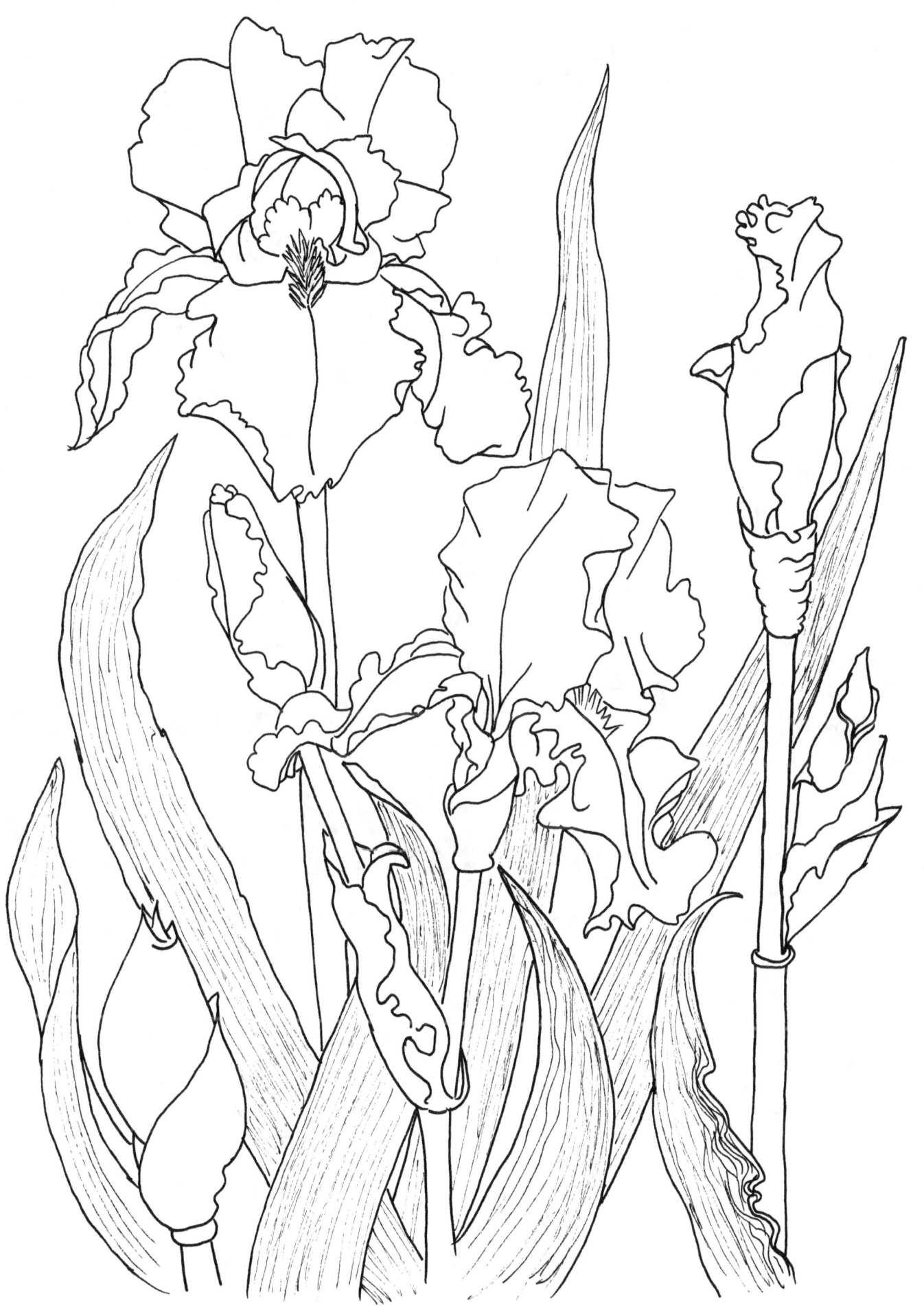

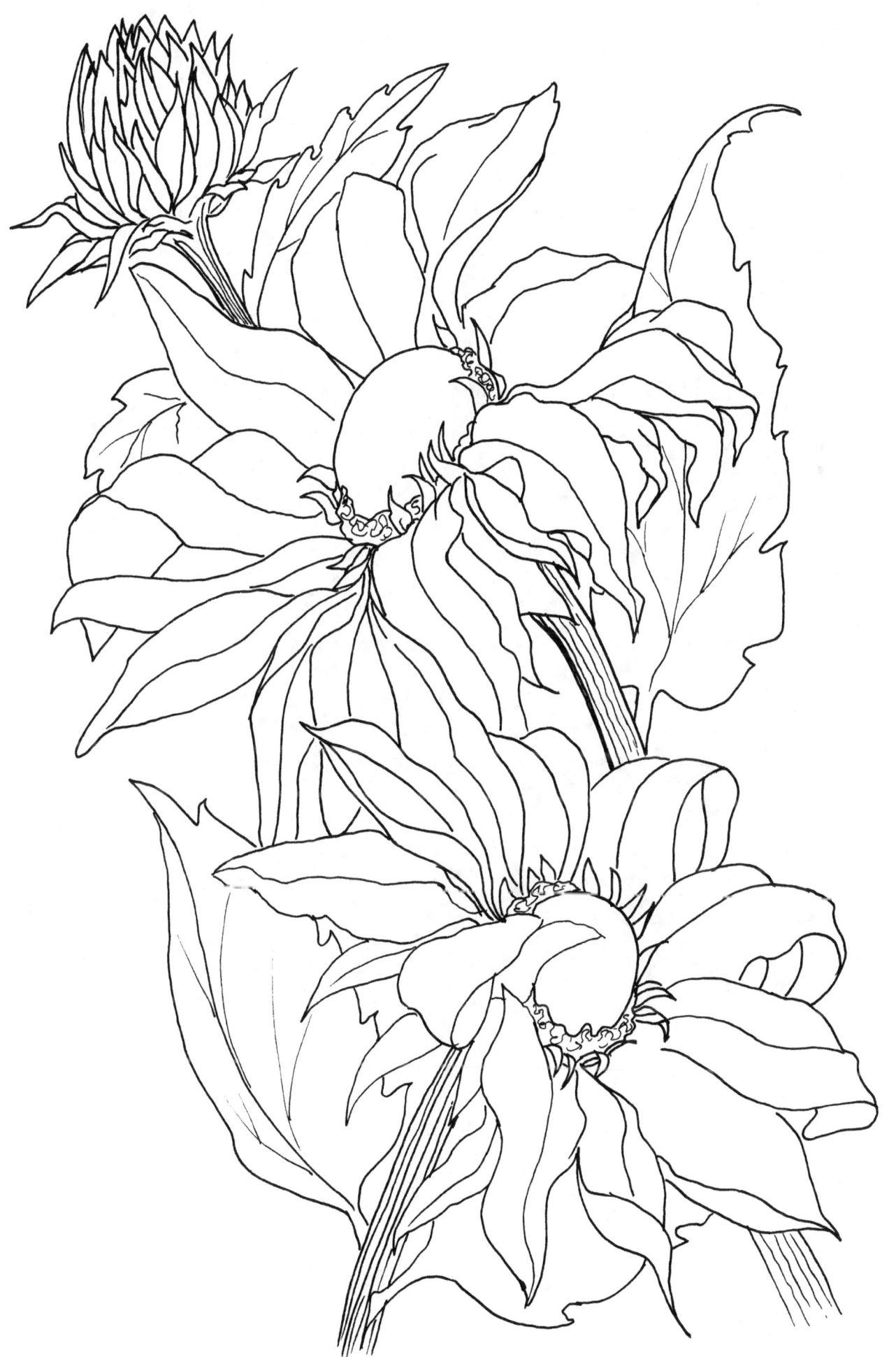

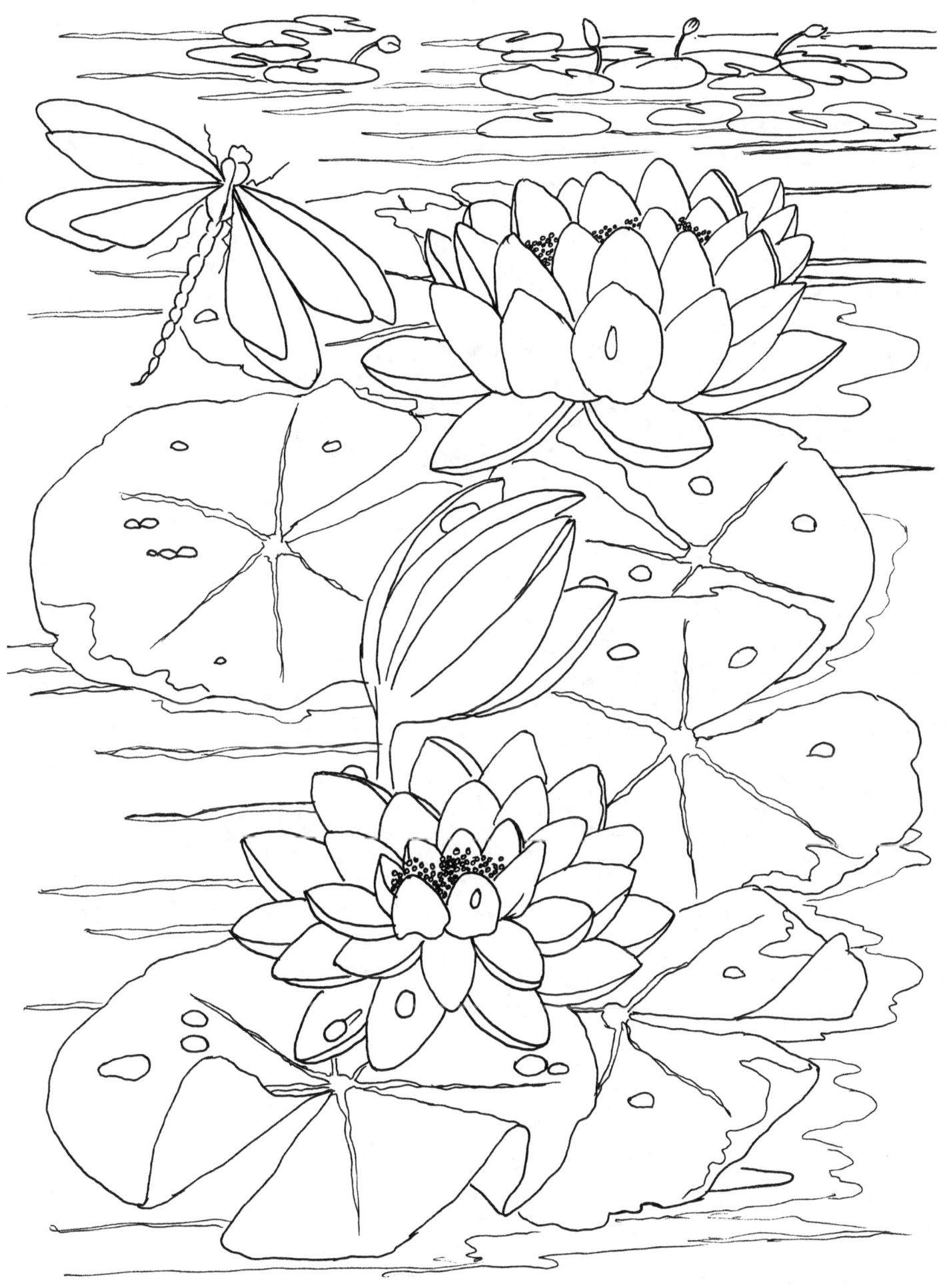

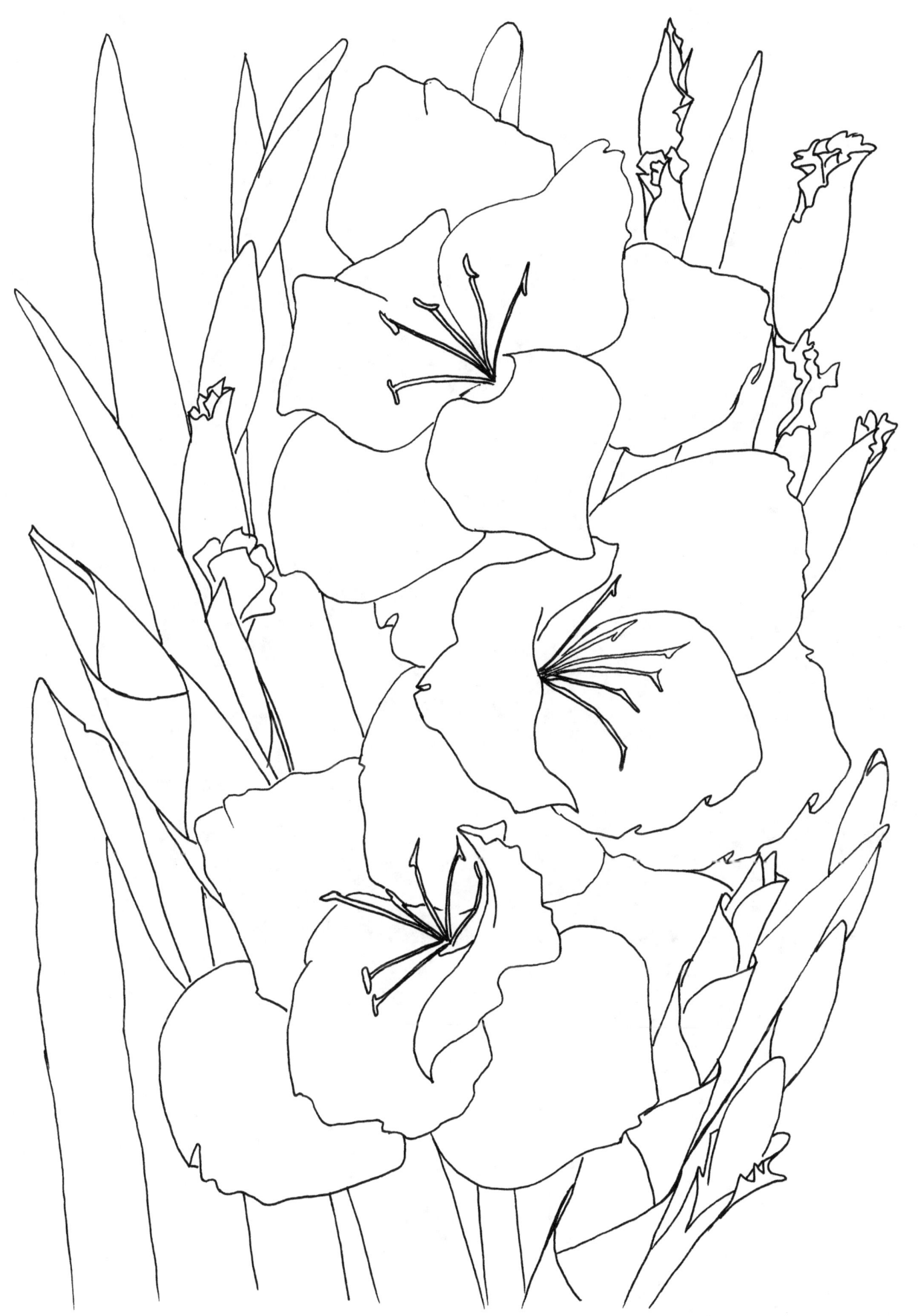

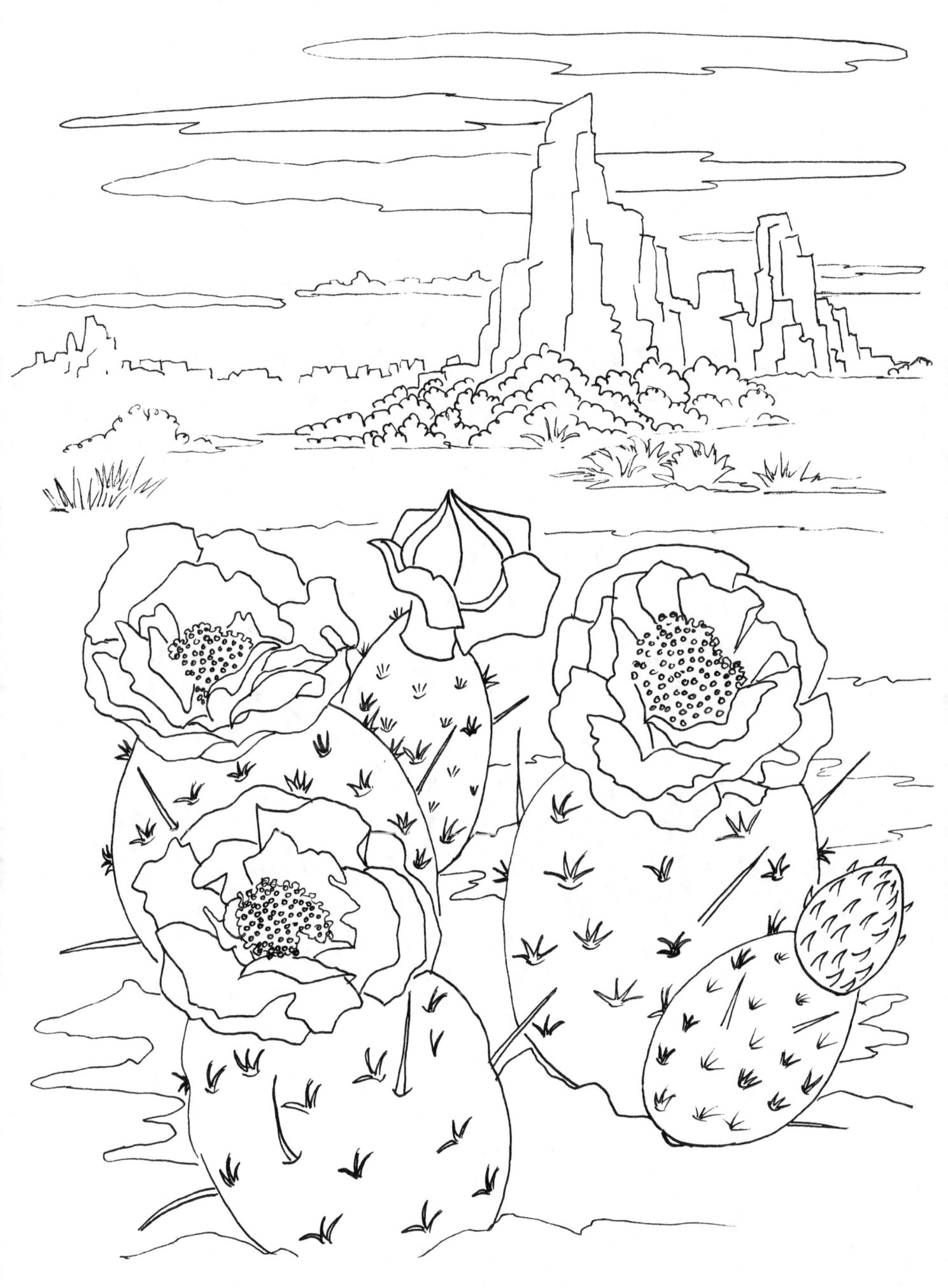

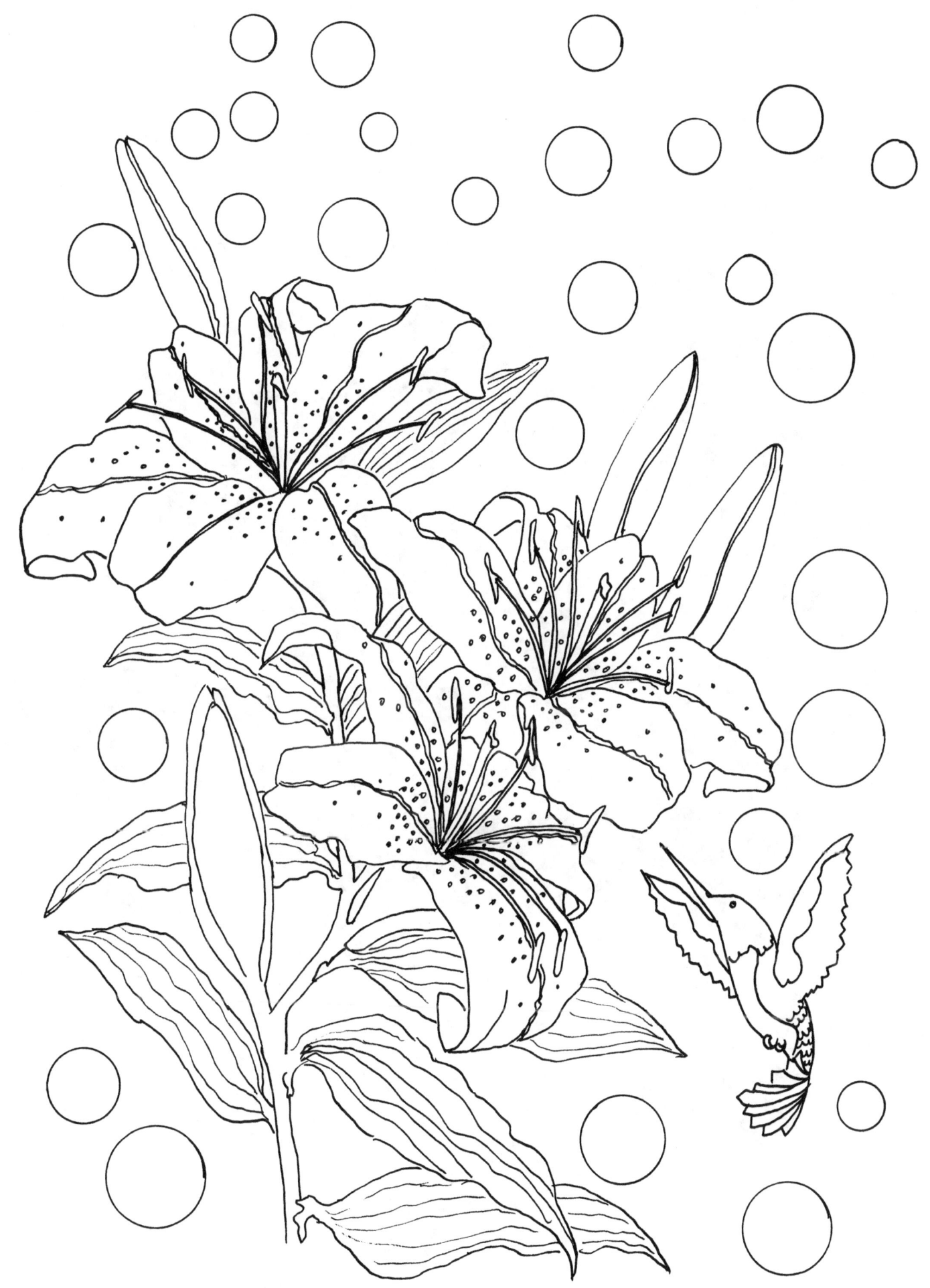

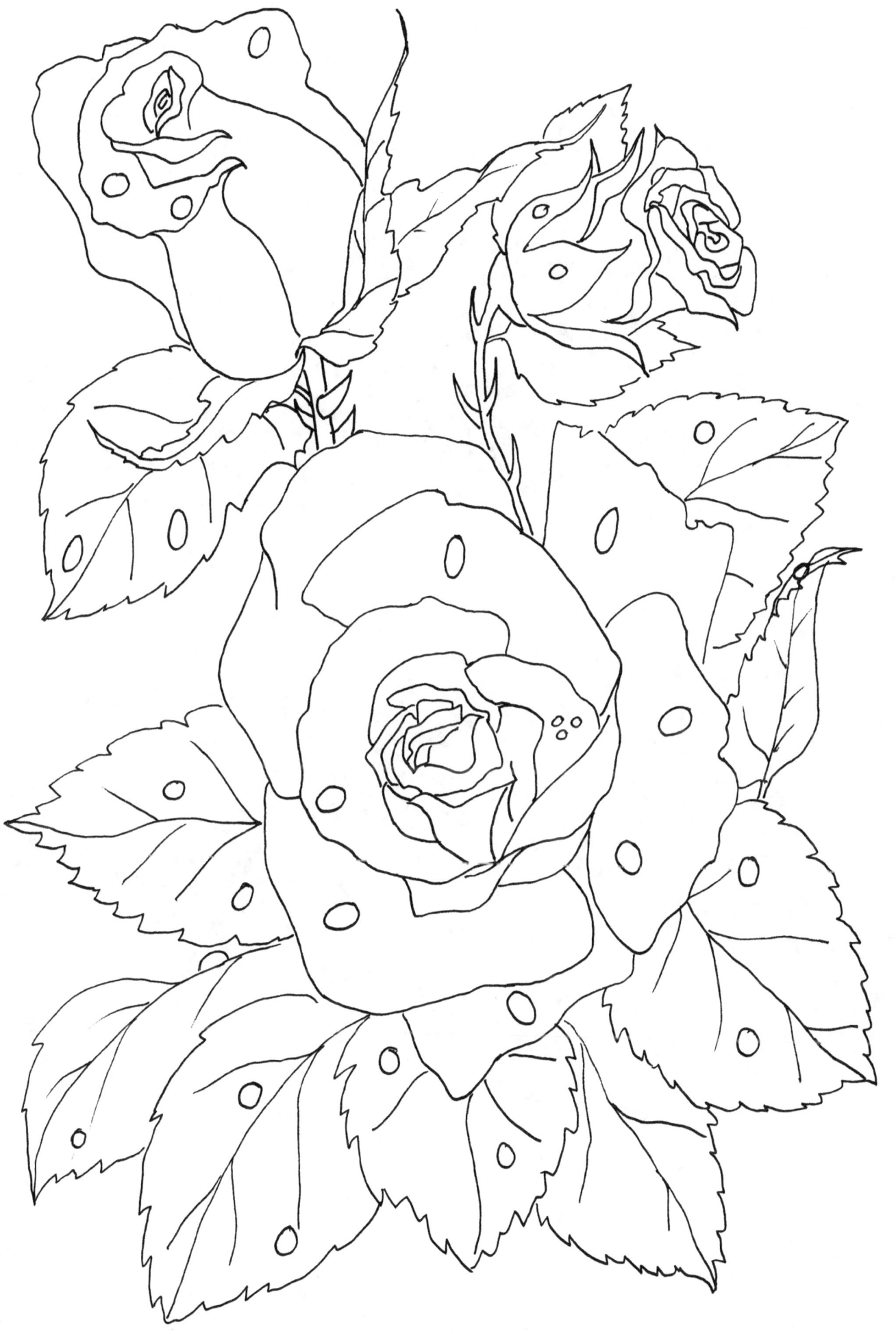

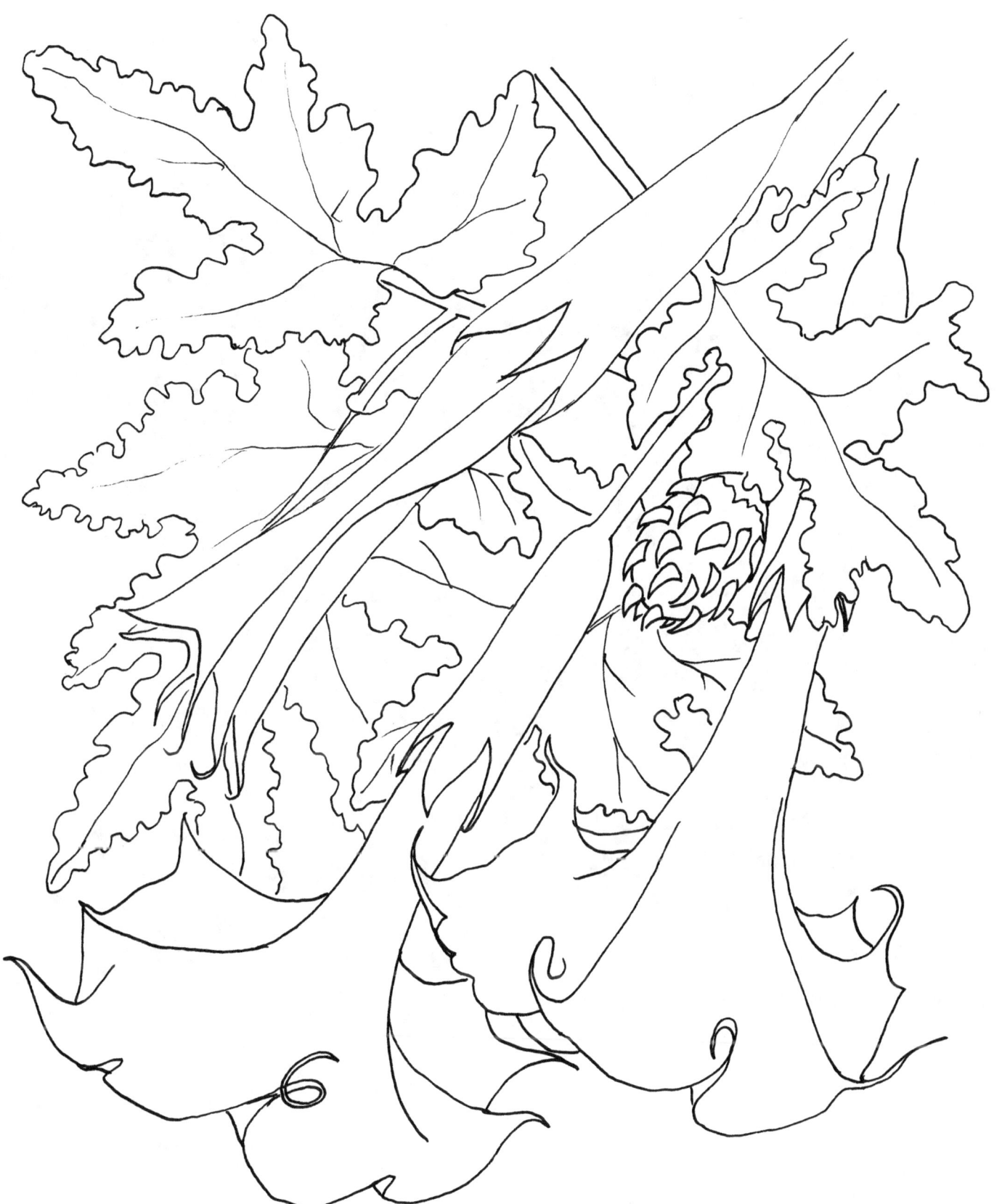

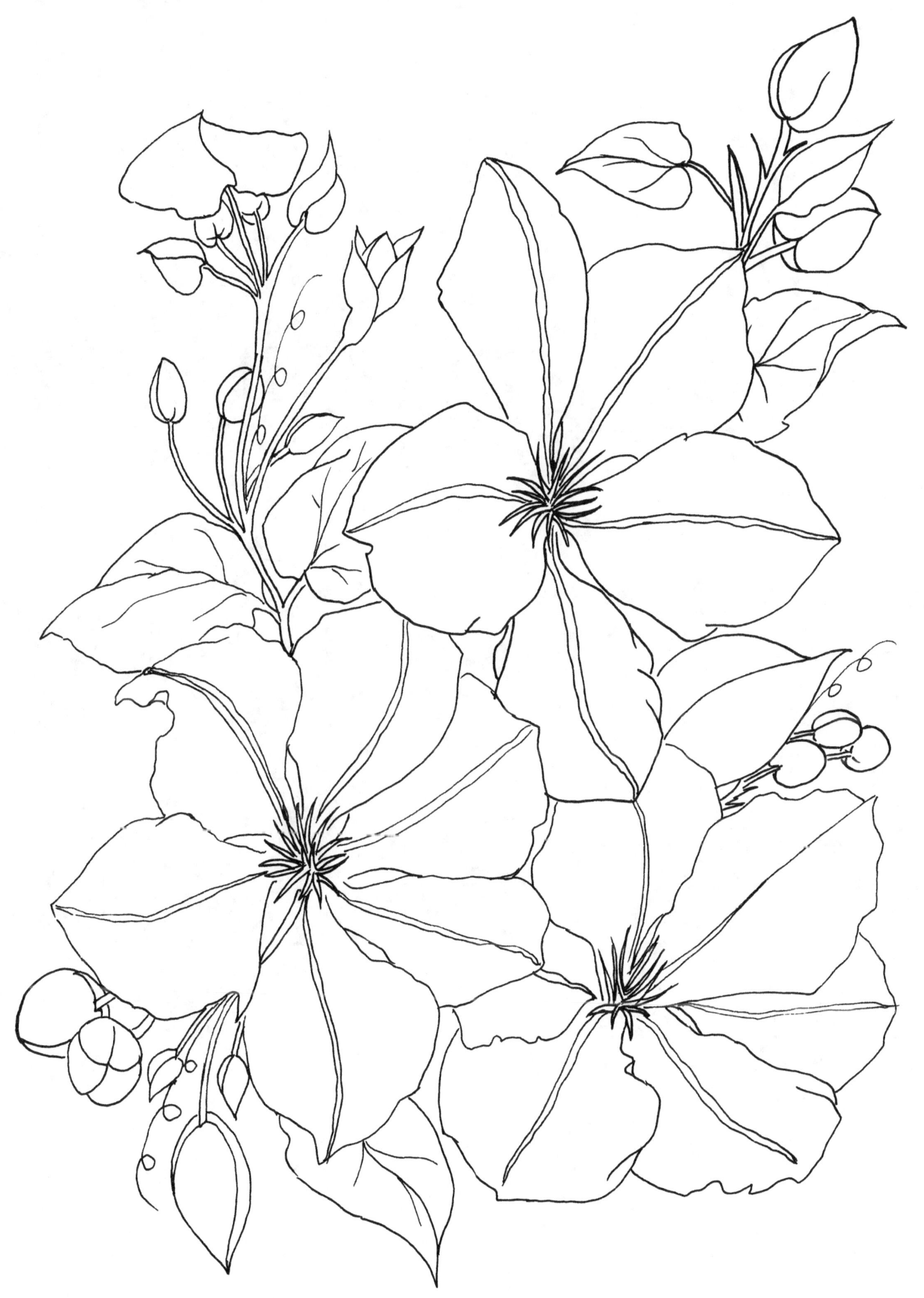

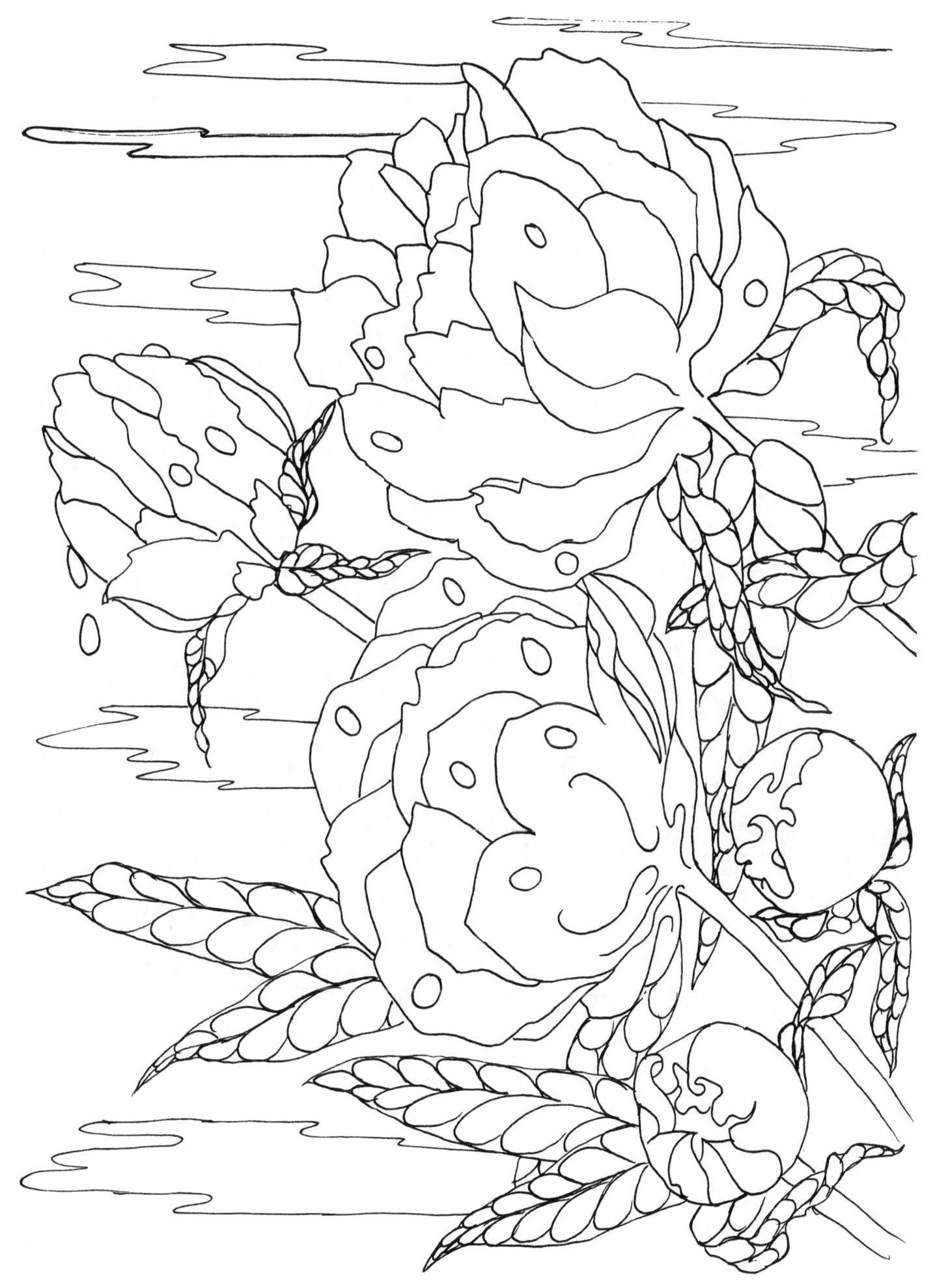

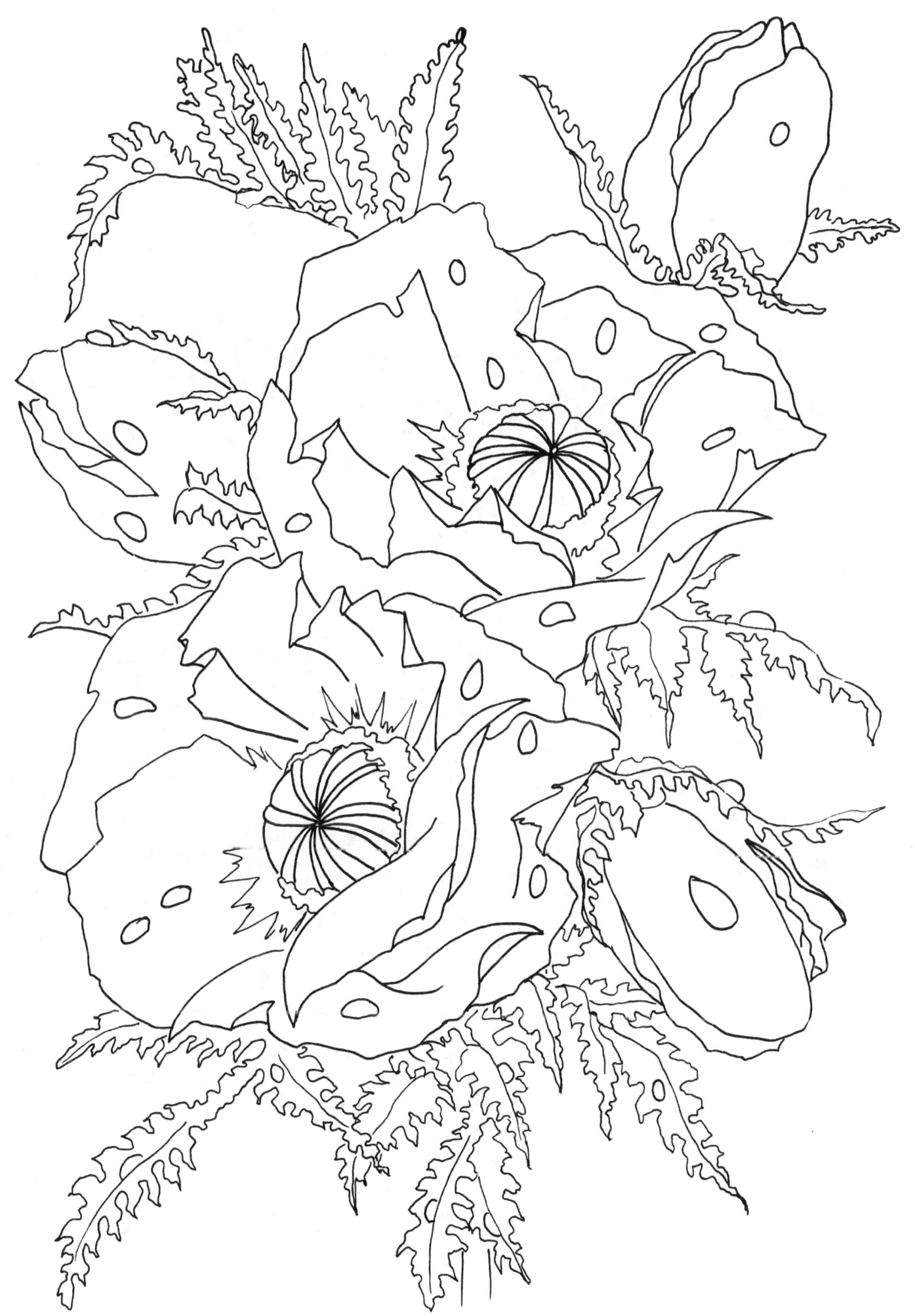

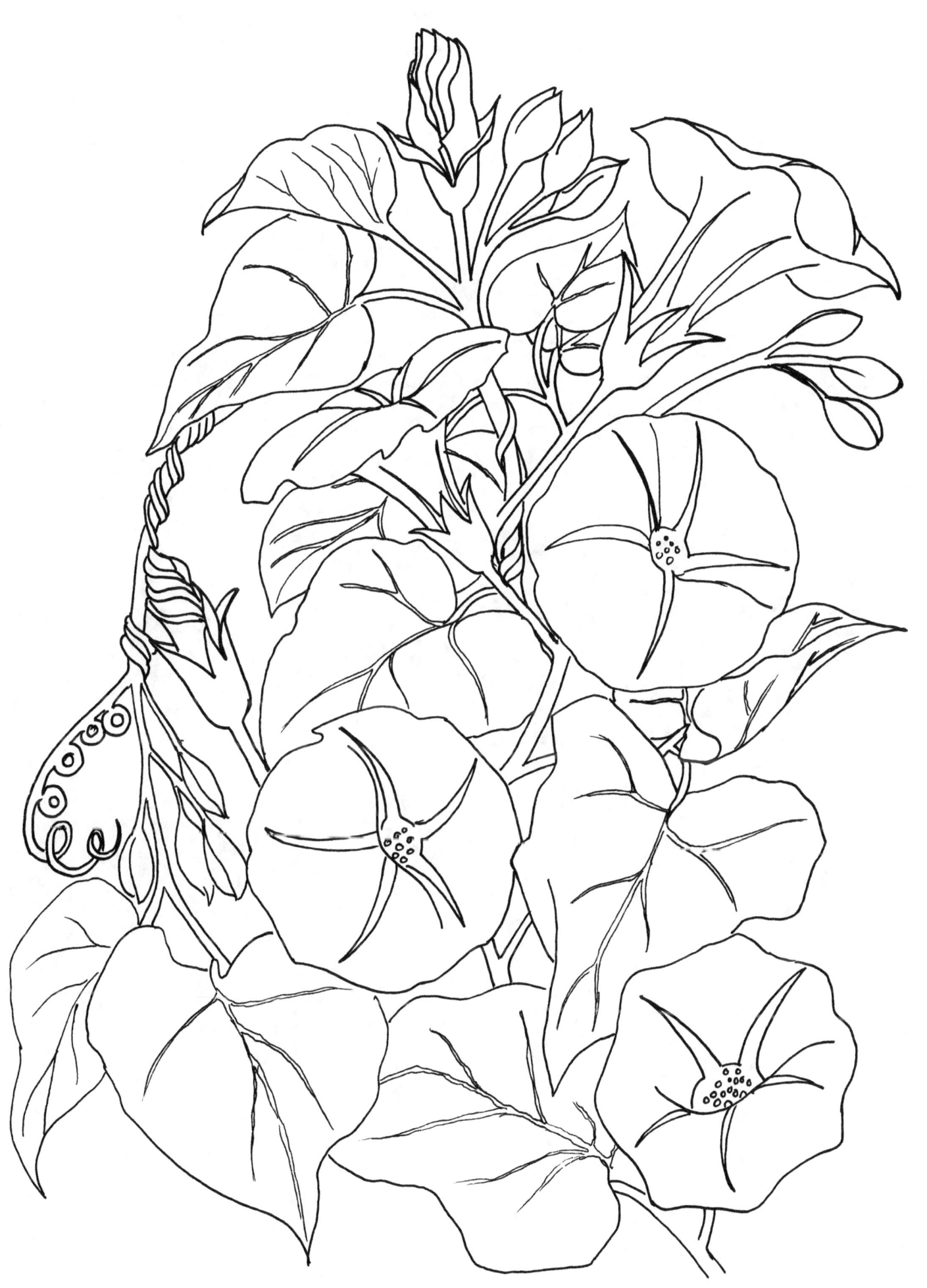

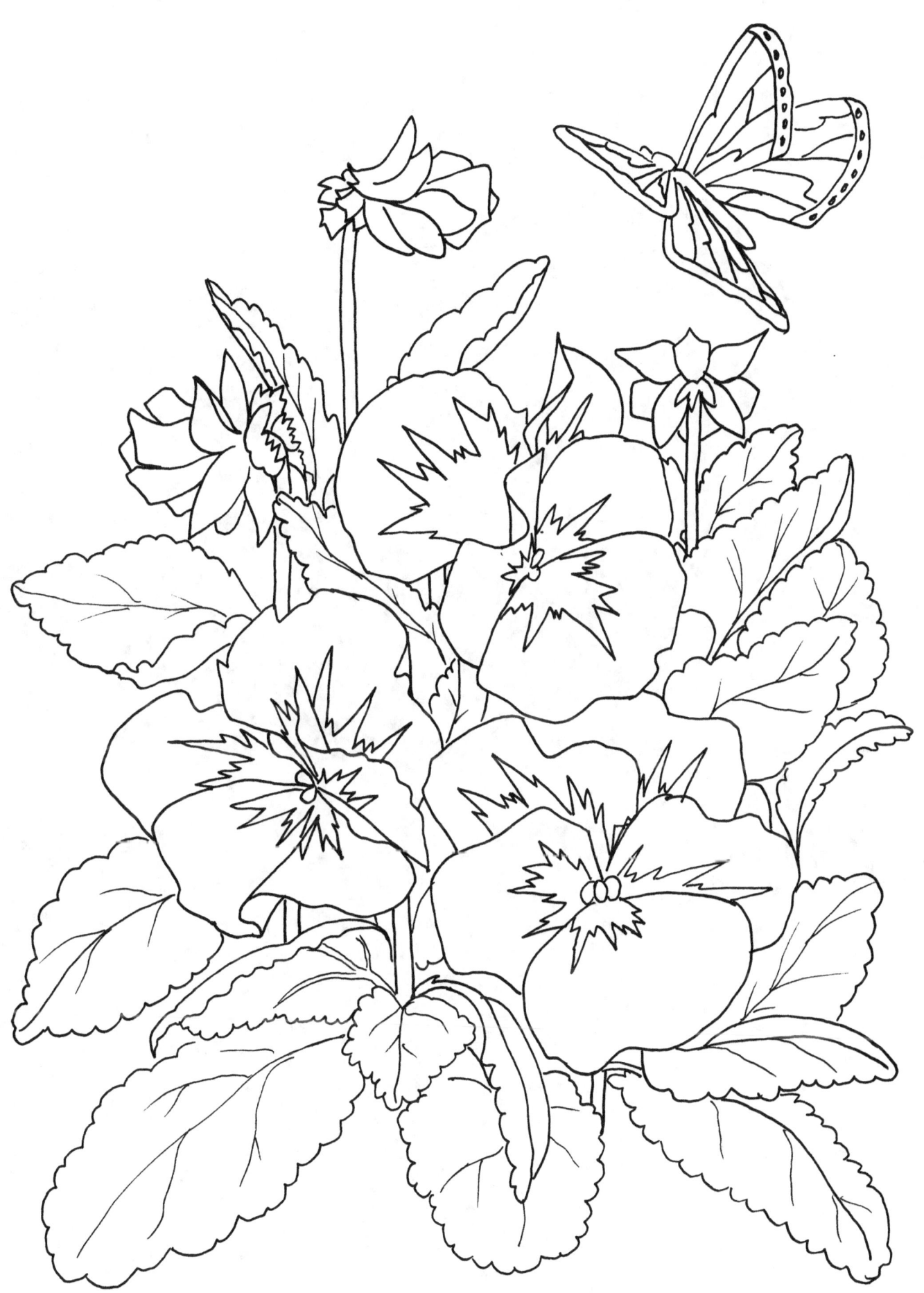

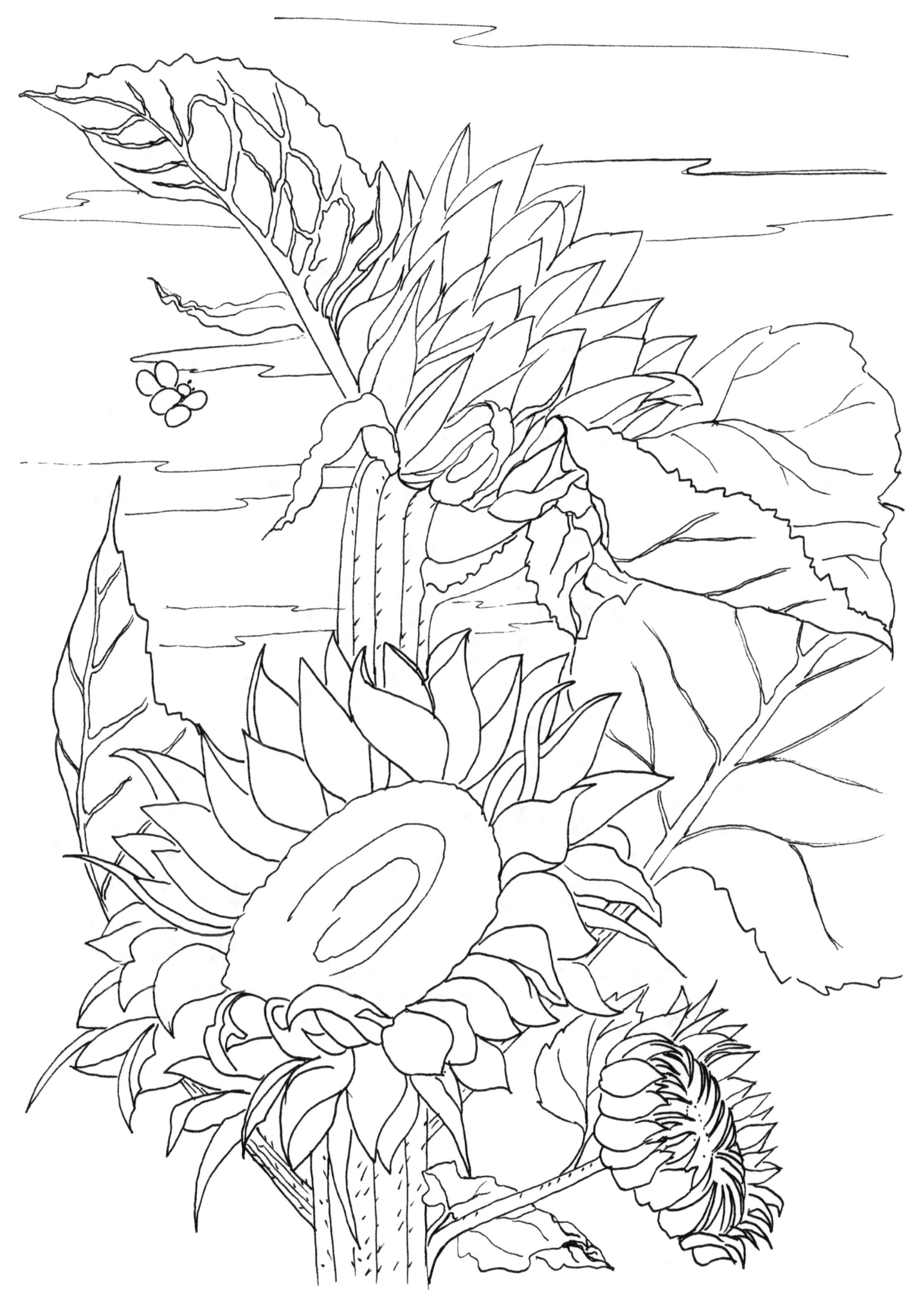

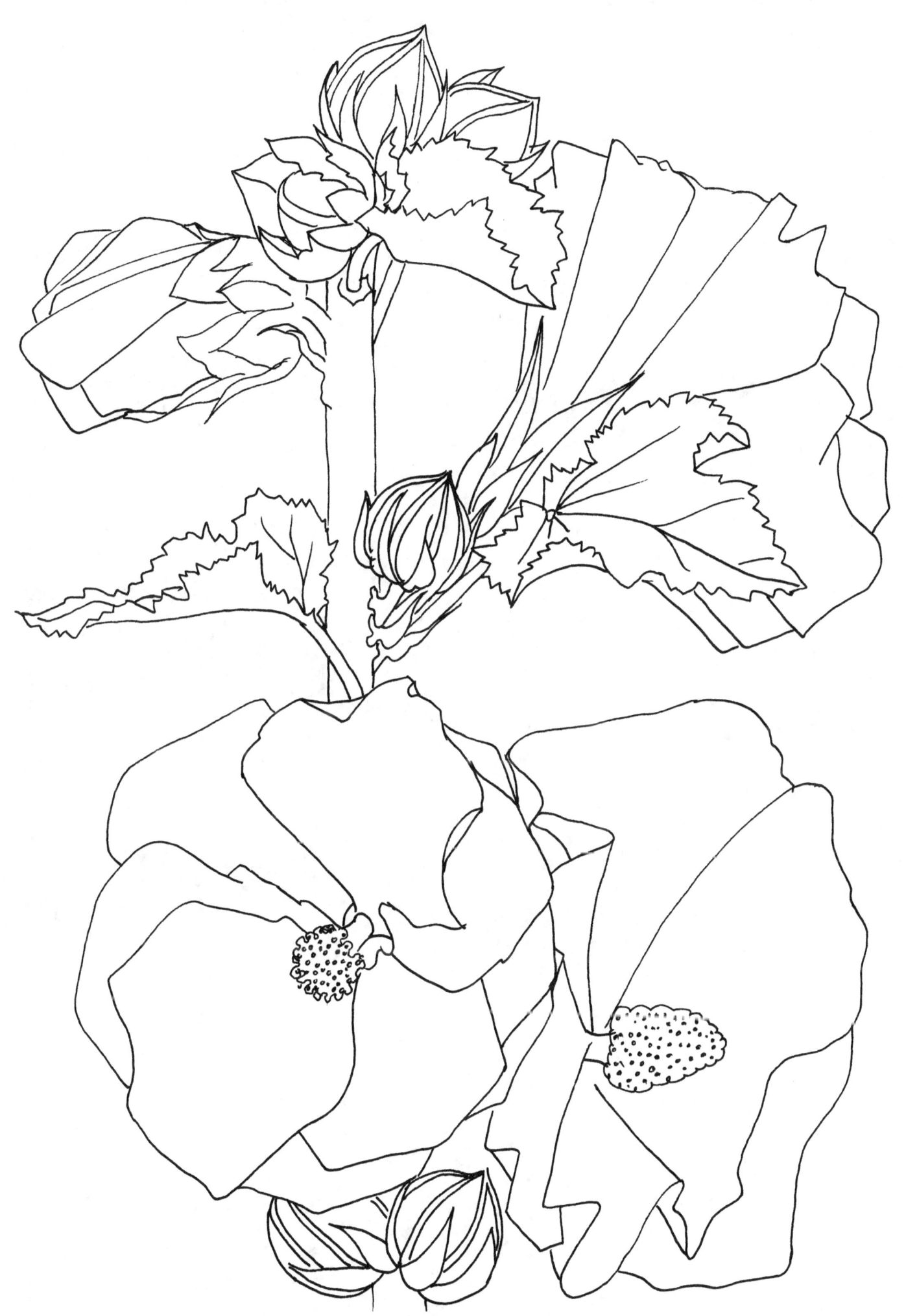

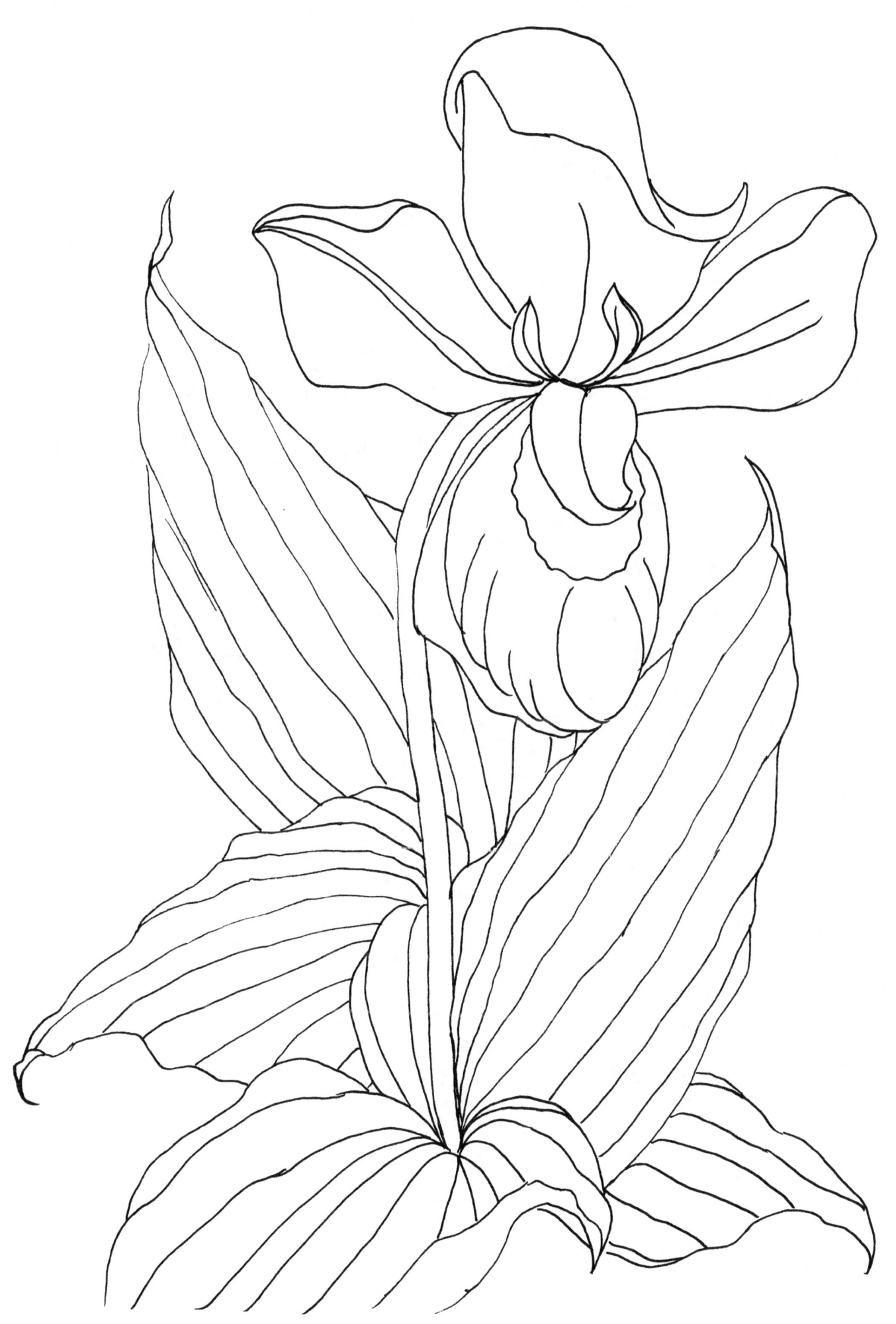

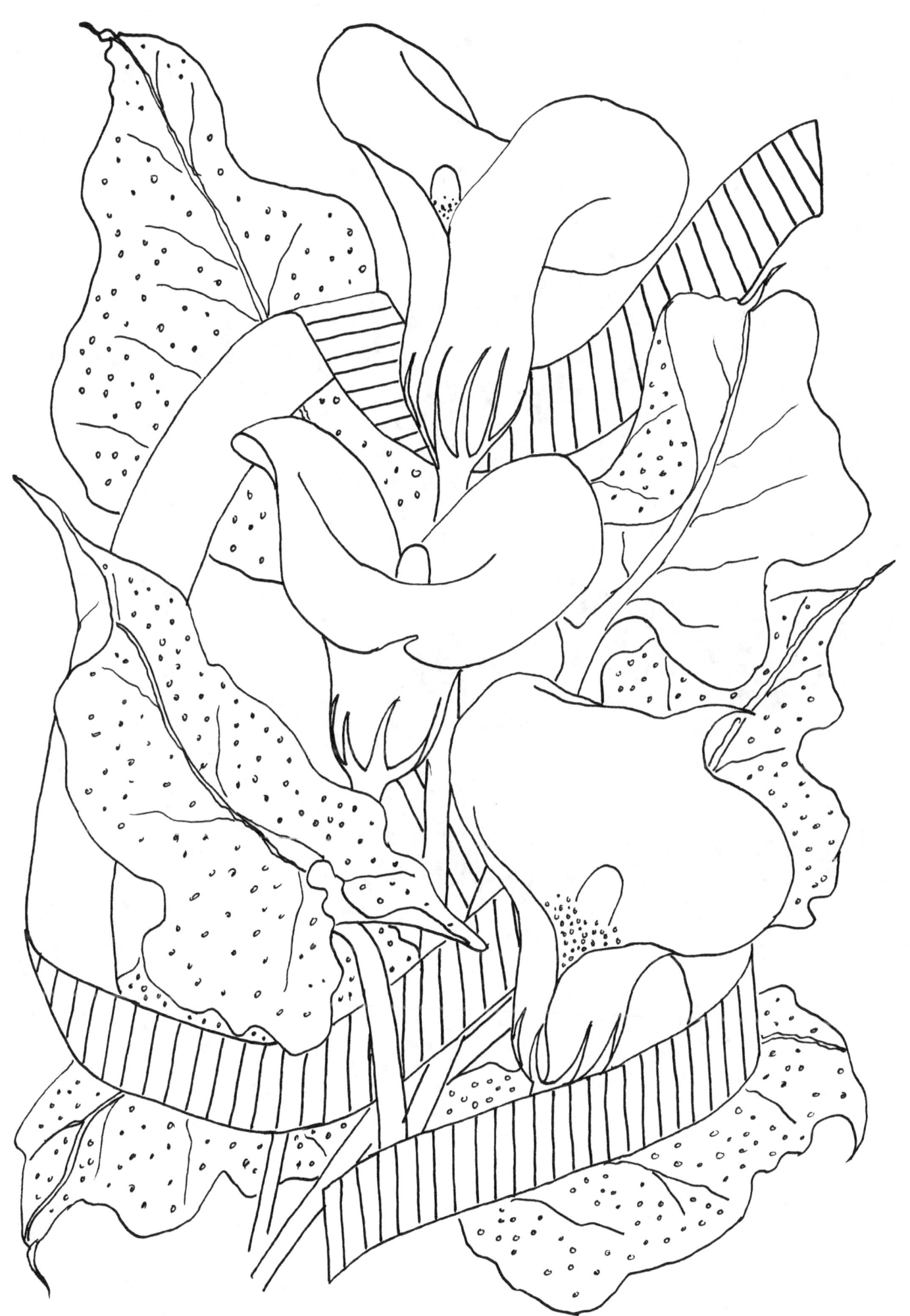

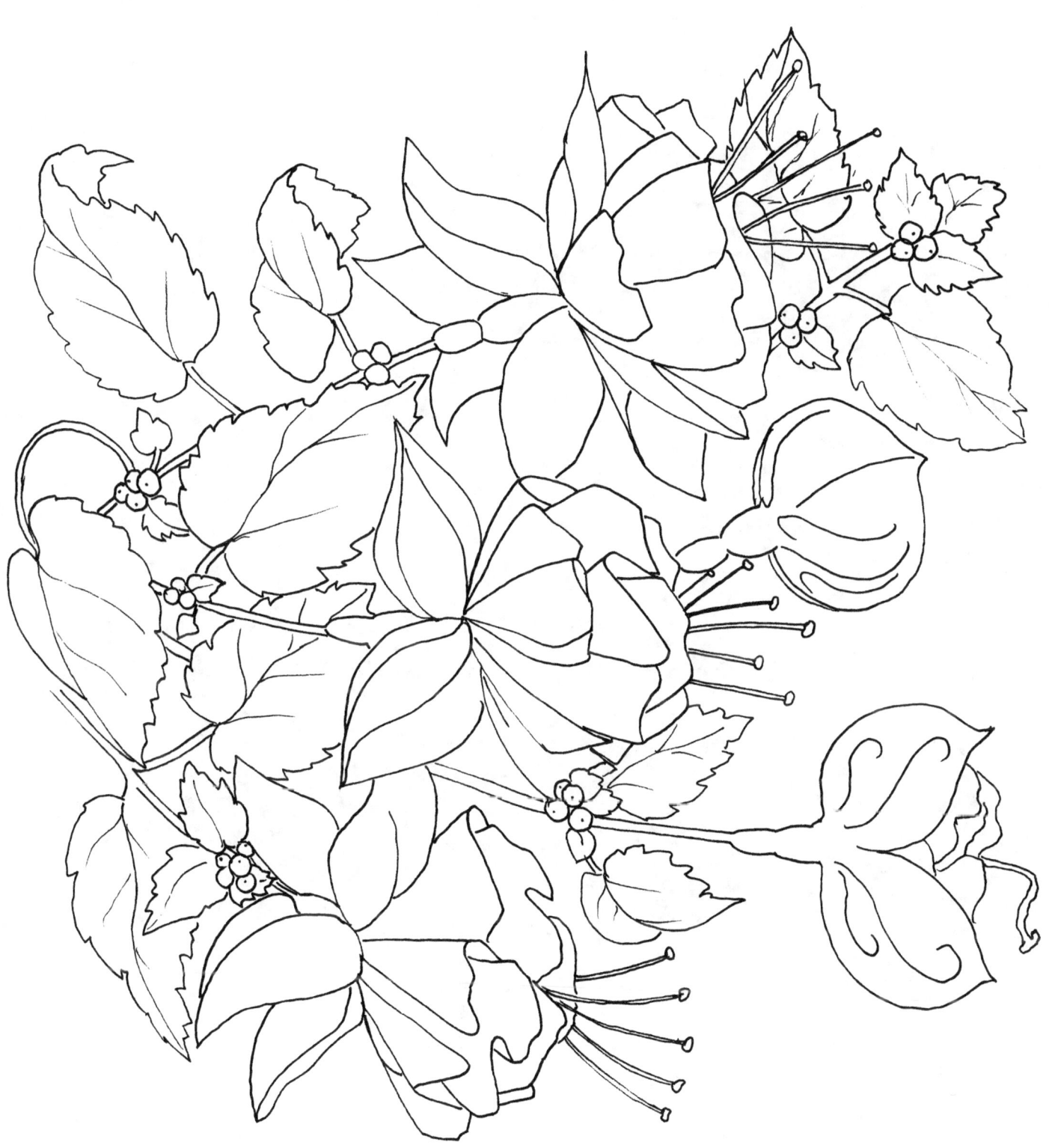

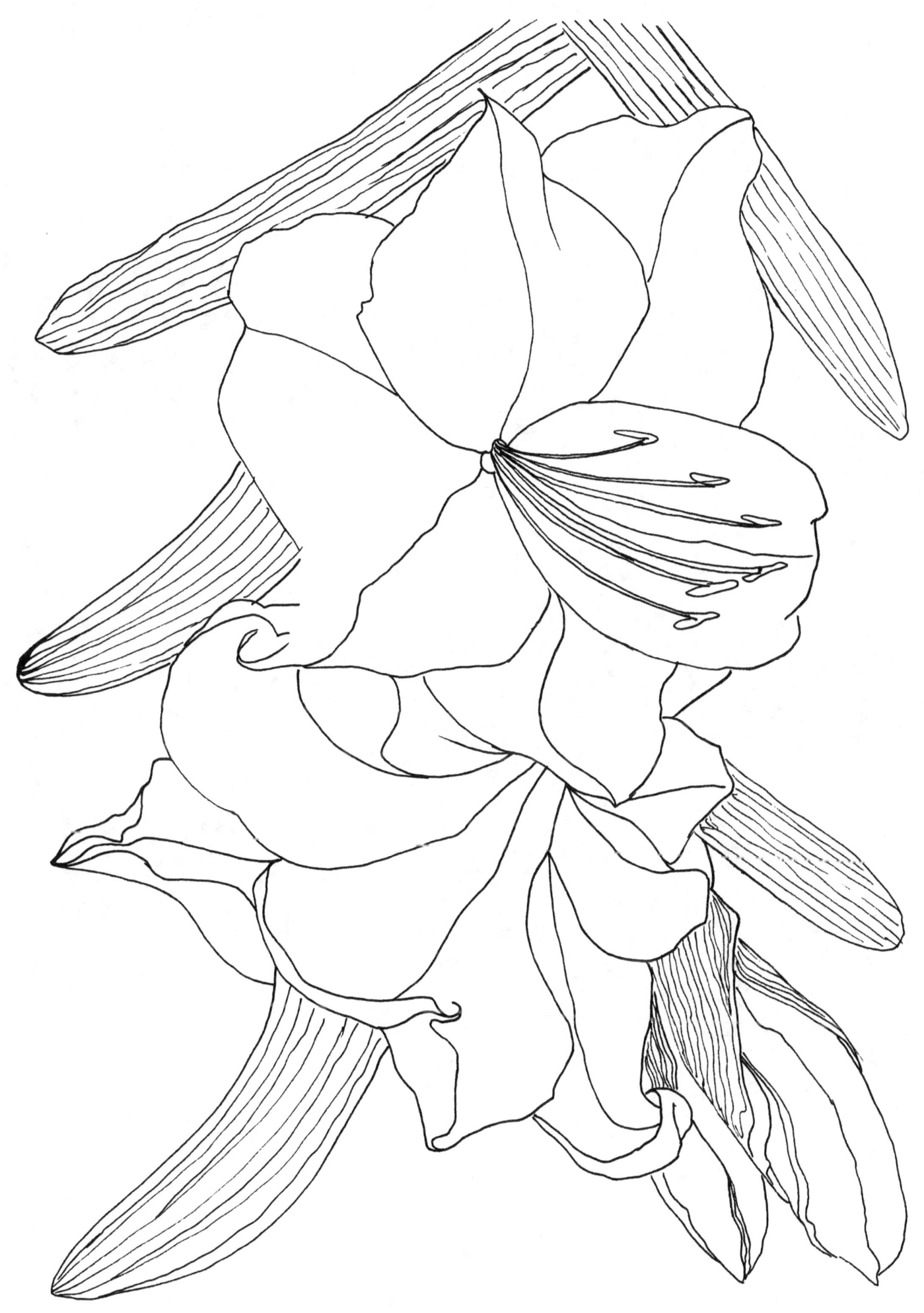

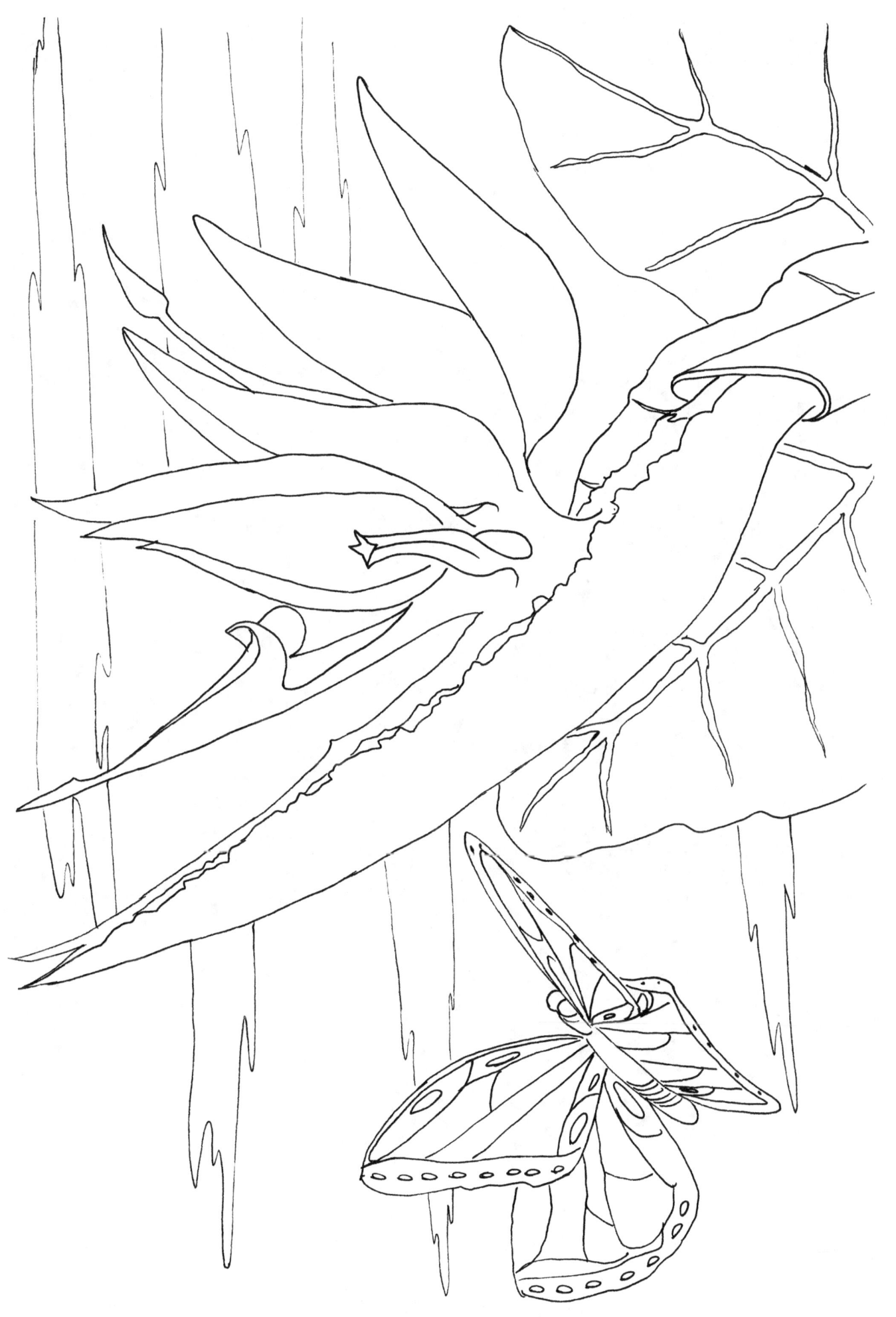

www.ingramcontent.com/pod-product-compliance
Lightning Source LLC
Chambersburg PA
CBHW081303180526
45170CB00007B/2541